Tom Thumb

Story written by Gill Munton
Illustrated by Tim Archbold

Speed Sounds

Consonants

Ask children to say the sounds.

f	l	m	n	r	s	v	z	sh	th	ng
ff	ll	mm	nn	rr	ss	ve	zz			nk
ph	(le)	(mb)	kn	(wr)	se		se			
					ce		s			

b	c	d	g	h	j	p	(qu)	t	w	x	y	ch
bb	k	dd	gg		g	pp		tt	wh			(tch)
	ck				ge							

Each box contains one sound but sometimes more than one grapheme.
*Focus graphemes for this story are **circled**.*

Vowels

Ask children to say the sounds in and out of order.

a	e ea	i	o	u	ay	ee y	igh i	ow o
at	hen	in	on	up	day	see	high	blow

oo	oo	ar	or oor ore	air	ir	ou	oy oi
zoo	look	car	for	fair	whirl	shout	boy

Story Green Words

Tom Thumb   in fact   thumb   wrong   gulp   bank   rod

string   chef*   guest*

Ask children to say the syllables and then read the whole word.

match|box   e|las|tic   in|sects   vel|vet   ban|quet   gob|let

splen|did   a|mong*

Ask children to read the root first and then the whole word with the suffix.

finch → finches   visit → visiting   spot → spotted

present → presented

* Challenge Words

Vocabulary Check

Discuss the meaning (as used in the story) after the children have read each word.

	definition:	**sentence:**
in fact	*actually, truly*	*In fact, he was no taller than a man's thumb.*
chatted to the finches	*talked to the birds*	*He chatted to the finches and frogs.*
spotted	*saw*	*a big fish spotted him jumping into the pond*
snack	*something to eat*	*Wanting a quick snack, it swam up to him.*
gulp	*a big swallow*	*and – gulp! – snapped him up!*
bank	*edge of the pond*	*A man was fishing from the bank with a ...*
rod	*stick with string to catch fish*	*... rod and a bit of string*

Red Words

Ask children to practise reading the words across the rows, down the columns and in and out of order clearly and quickly.

small	was	to	do
said	of	what	small
their	do	all	was
what	your	saw	watch
they	are	school	me

Tom Thumb

Tom Thumb was small.
In fact, he was no bigger than a man's thumb.

His bed was a matchbox
and his bath was an eggcup.

His cap was a button,
his belt was an elastic band,
and his jacket was lent to him by a doll.

He skipped with the insects,
and he chatted to the finches
and the frogs.

It was when Tom Thumb was visiting the frogs
that things went badly wrong.

A big fish spotted him jumping into the pond.
It swam up to him, and gulp!
It snapped him up!

"Help!" yelled Tom Thumb, from the fish's tummy.

A man was fishing from the bank
with a rod and a bit of string.
When he pulled in the string,
a big fish was on the end of it.

Off he went to sell the fish
to the King's chef.

In his kitchen, the King's chef cut the fish up.
He must have felt shocked when out stepped ...
Tom Thumb!!

"What can I do with this
little chap?"
the chef said to himself.
He had a think.
Then he popped Tom Thumb
into the King's plum pudding!

When the pudding was cut, out stepped ... Tom Thumb!

He jumped into the King's dish,
crossed his legs and grinned at the King.

The King clapped and clapped.

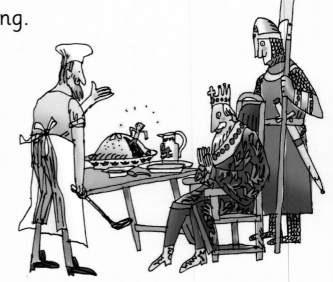

"Thank you!" he said to the chef,
and handed him a big bag of gold.
"What a splendid little chap!
He can do tricks for my guests when I have a banquet!"

So the King kept Tom Thumb.
He dressed him in velvet and silk,
and presented him with a little tin drum.

When the King had a banquet,
Tom Thumb banged on his drum
and did tricks for the guests.

The guests clapped, and lifted their goblets,
saying "Let's all drink to Tom Thumb!"

Questions to talk about

Ask children to TTYP each question using 'Fastest finger' (FF) or 'Have a think' (HaT).

p.9 (FF) Where did Tom Thumb sleep? Where did he wash?

p.10 (FF) What did he wear? Who were his friends?

p.11 (FF) How did things go badly wrong?

p.12 (FF) Who is the man going to sell his fish to?

p.13 (HaT) How do you think Tom Thumb felt when he was in the kitchen?

p.14 (HaT) Why does the King give the chef a bag of gold?

p.15 (FF) What did Tom have to do for the King and his guests?

Questions to read and answer

(Children complete without your help.)

1. Tom Thumb was **very big / very small**.

2. Things went wrong when Tom was visiting **the fish / the frogs / the birds**.

3. Tom Thumb was in **a cat's tummy / a fish's tummy / a frog's tummy**.

4. The chef put Tom Thumb in **the King's bed / the King's plum pudding / the King's drink**.

5. The chef got a big bag of **gold / sand / fish**.

Speedy Green Words

Ask children to practise reading the words across the rows, down the columns and in and out of order clearly and quickly.

bath	end	sell	himself
kitchen	king	bath	end
fish	bed	when	box
have	wrong	badly	bigger
this	little	cut	out